KNITTING
TIPS & TECHNIQUES

Publications International, Ltd.

Consulting by Zee Wang

Written by Beth Taylor

Photo styling by Maire Phelan

Photography by Christopher Hiltz
Additional photography from Shutterstock.com

Knitting symbols and abbreviations from Craft Yarn Council's www.YarnStandards.com

Louis Weber, CEO
Publications International, Ltd.
8140 Lehigh Avenue
Morton Grove, IL 60053

ISBN: 978-1-63938-507-2

Manufactured in China.

8 7 6 5 4 3 2 1

Let's get social!
 @Publications_International
 @PublicationsInternational
www.pilbooks.com

CONTENTS

All About Yarn

Yarn is simply the continuous strand of twisted fiber with which you will knit. Yarns come in a variety of fibers, textures, and weights (thicknesses). Explore the offerings at your local yarn or craft store, or peruse the options at online retailers.

Yarn for Beginners

For beginning knitters learning the basics, select a smooth, sturdy yarn that is medium (worsted) weight and light colored. It's harder to see your stitches with dark colored yarn. Avoid fuzzy and loosely woven yarns that split easily.

Yarn Fibers

Yarn is made from all sorts of fibers, both natural and synthetic. You'll also find yarns made from a mix of natural and synthetic fibers, and in every combination imaginable.

Natural fibers include those made from plant fibers (cotton, linen, and hemp) as well as those made from animal fibers (wool, silk, cashmere, mohair, alpaca, and angora). Yarns made from plant fibers are lightweight, breathable, and machine washable. Yarns made from animal fibers are warmer than plant fiber yarns. Both types of natural fibers offer a bit of stretch.

Synthetic fibers include nylon, rayon, acrylic, and polyester. Synthetic yarns are usually less expensive than natural fibers, but are less breathable and pill more easily.

Novelty and specialty yarns include bouclé, ladder, eyelash, faux fur, and chenille. While great for trims and accessories, novelty yarn is not best for beginners.

Purchasing Your Yarn

Each package of store-bought yarn has a label (or ball band) listing the yarn's length, fiber content, and weight. Yarn weight refers to the thickness of a yarn. It ranges from the thinnest embroidery thread to the bulkiest yarn. Yarn package labels also recommend knitting needle size—just look for the knitting needles symbol to find the U.S. and metric (mm) needle size. Yarn labels also list the color, including dye lot. Purchase enough yarn to knit your project, plus some extra in case of mistakes, from the same dye lot. Always save at least one label from your yarn and keep it where you can easily find it.

Yarn Weight Guidelines

LACE

Yarn types: Fingering, lace, and 10-count crochet thread

Recommended metric needle sizes: 1.5–2.25 mm

Recommended U.S. needle sizes: 000 to 1

Knit gauge range: 33–40 stitches to 4 in.

FINE

Yarn types: Sport and baby

Recommended metric needle sizes: 3.25–3.75 mm

Recommended U.S. needle sizes: 3 to 5

Knit gauge range: 23–26 stitches to 4 in.

MEDIUM

Yarn types: Afghan, aran, and worsted

Recommended metric needle sizes: 4.5–5.5 mm

Recommended U.S. needle sizes: 7 to 9

Knit gauge range: 16–20 stitches to 4 in.

SUPER BULKY

Yarn types: Super bulky and roving

Recommended metric needle sizes: 8–12.75 mm

Recommended U.S. needle sizes: 11 to 17

Knit gauge range: 7–11 stitches to 4 in.

SUPER FINE

Yarn types: Sock, fingering, and baby

Recommended metric needle sizes: 2.25–3.25 mm

Recommended U.S. needle sizes: 1 to 3

Knit gauge range: 27–32 stitches to 4 in.

LIGHT

Yarn types: Double knitting (DK) and light worsted

Recommended metric needle sizes: 3.75–4.5 mm

Recommended U.S. needle sizes: 5 to 7

Knit gauge range: 21–24 stitches to 4 in.

BULKY

Yarn types: Chunky, craft, and rug

Recommended metric needle sizes: 5.5–8 mm

Recommended U.S. needle sizes: 9 to 11

Knit gauge range: 12–15 stitches to 4 in.

JUMBO

Yarn types: Jumbo and roving

Recommended metric needle sizes: 12.75 mm and larger

Recommended U.S. needle sizes: 17 and larger

Knit gauge range: 6 stitches and fewer to 4 in.

Knitting Needles

Knitting needles come in three forms: straight (or single-point), circular, and double-pointed (or double-point). Knitting needles can be made from aluminum, plastic, wood, or bamboo. They are available in a wide range of sizes. Patterns will specify the type and size to use. Beginners should start with a pair of straight bamboo or wood needles no longer than 12".

Straight Needles

Straight or single-point needles have a point at one end and a knob on the other end to prevent your stitches from sliding off the needle. Straight needles are sold in pairs of various lengths, with 10" and 14" being the most common.

Circular Needles

Circular needles have a point at either end connected with a long, flexible cord. Use circular needles for knitting tubular pieces in the round or for flat pieces in back-and-forth knitting (especially useful for large items with too many stitches to fit on a straight needle).

Double-Pointed Needles (dpn)

Double-pointed (or double-point) needles have points on both ends. Use double-pointed needles to knit small pieces in the round, turn sock heels, and make I-cords. Double-pointed needles are typically sold in sets of four or five.

Cable Needles (cn)

Cable needles are short, double-pointed needles with a curve in the center. These are used in cable knitting. You'll temporarily slip one set of stitches onto the cable needle while working another set of stitches, creating a twisted effect.

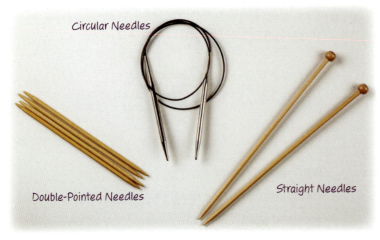

Circular Needles

Double-Pointed Needles

Straight Needles

U.S. Size	Metric (Millimeter) Size Range
000	1.5 mm
00	1.75 mm
0	2 mm
1	2.25 mm
2	2.75 mm
3	3.125–3.25 mm
4	3.5 mm
5	3.75 mm
6	4–4.25 mm
7	4.5 mm
8	5 mm
9	5.25–5.5 mm
10	5.75–6 mm
10½	6.5 mm
11	8 mm
13	9 mm
15	10 mm
17	12.5–12.75 mm
19	15 mm
35	19 mm
50	25 mm
70	35 mm

Other Supplies

In addition to yarn and needles, here are some other handy supplies for knitting.

Scissors

Using sharp scissors to cut yarn will prevent fraying and keep your edges clean. Try fabric shears for cutting thick yarns or multiple strands, or embroidery scissors for trimming yarn tails close to your work.

Tapestry Needles

Tapestry or yarn needles have a blunt tip and an eye large enough to accommodate thick yarns. Use these special needles to weave in yarn tails or sew knitted pieces together.

Stitch Markers

As their name suggests, stitch markers are designed to mark your stitches. Use them to mark a certain number of stitches, the beginning of a round, or where to make a particular stitch. Closed stitch markers are placed over a needle tip. Locking stitch markers look like mini safety pins and can be opened and closed. Split markers have a little slit in the ring so you can place the marker into a stitch rather than onto a needle tip. Purchase stitch markers, or improvise with pins, earrings, or safety pins.

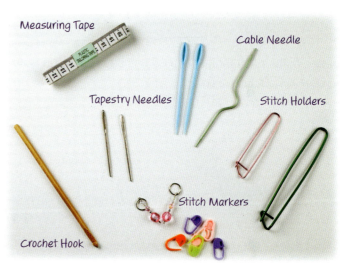

Measurement Tools

Use a tape measure, stitch gauge, or ruler to measure your gauge. You'll need a tape measure, marked with inches and centimeters, to take body measurements before making garments.

Crochet Hooks

Use a crochet hook to make decorative edgings and fringe, and to fix dropped stitches. Just like knitting needles, crochet hooks come in bamboo, wood, aluminum, or plastic. They have a U.S. and metric (mm) size.

Stitch Holders

These gigantic safety pins are designed to hold open stitches until you're ready to pick them up again. This prevents your stitches from unraveling. If you don't have a stitch holder, thread a length of yarn or cord through the open stitches and tie the ends.

Pins

Use long, rustproof pins for blocking and pinning seams together. Pins can also serve as stitch markers. Choose pins with large, colorful heads made of glass or plastic for pinning seams together (plastic heads can melt under the intense heat of an iron) and rustproof T-pins for blocking.

Slip Knot

The first step in knitting is a slip knot. The slip knot is what attaches the yarn to the needle and what makes casting on possible. The slip knot counts as the first stitch in the cast-on row.

Make a circle with the yarn so the tail end is on bottom and the working yarn (the yarn coming from the ball) is on top.

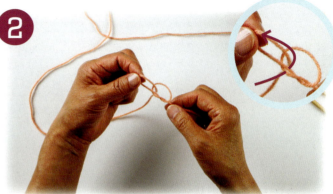

Make a separate loop with the working yarn and pull it from behind and up through the circle you made in step 1.

Pull the loop and the yarn tail in opposite directions to complete the slip knot.

Insert the needle from right to left through the slip knot loop. Pull the tail and the working yarn to tighten the slip knot snug against the needle. You are now ready to cast on.

Cast On (CO)

The cast-on row is the foundation of knitting. There are many ways to cast on stitches. Try the following cast-on methods, and experiment until you find what feels most comfortable. The cast-on stitches should be loose and elastic enough to allow the needle back into those stitches for the next row. If you find your cast-on stitches are too tight, try casting on with two needles held together or using a needle two or three sizes larger than you'll use for the remainder of the project.

Knitted Cast-On

The knitted cast-on uses two needles. This method is good when you need a firm edge. Work loosely, without pulling the stitches too tight.

1

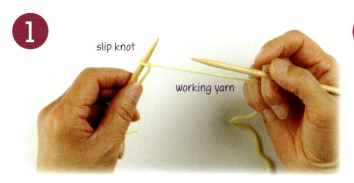

slip knot

working yarn

Start with a slip knot on the needle in your left hand, holding the yarn tail out of the way. Hold the empty needle in your right hand, with the working yarn (the yarn coming from the ball) behind the needle.

2

Insert the right needle through the stitch (the slip knot) on the left needle. The needles should form an X, with the right needle under the left needle. The yarn tail is on the left and the working yarn is on the right.

3

Wrap the working yarn around the right needle from back to front and bottom to top, ending between the needles.

4

With the right needle, draw that working yarn back through the stitch on the left needle, creating a new loop on the right needle. The left needle is now under the right needle.

5

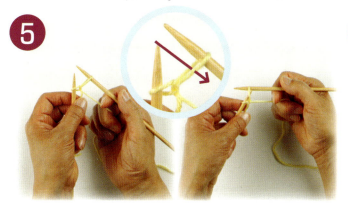

Insert the tip of the left needle into the new loop, transferring the new loop from the right needle to the left needle.

6

There are 2 loops on the left needle (slip knot + cast-on stitch just made = 2 cast-on stitches). Repeat steps 2–5 for each additional cast-on stitch until reaching the required number of cast-on stitches.

9

Long-Tail Cast-On

The long-tail cast-on (also called the slingshot cast-on) is a popular method that creates an elastic edge. Both the working yarn and tail are used, so you'll need an extra-long tail before you start. The tail length should be about three times the width of your desired cast-on, or about one inch per stitch.

1

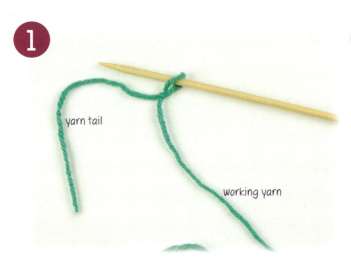

Make a slip knot with an extra-long tail and place it on the needle as shown. Hold the needle in your right hand. Coming from behind with left palm facing, separate the strands with your left thumb and index finger so the tail is draped over your thumb and the working yarn over your index finger.

2

Wrap the working yarn over your left index finger and the tail around your left thumb. Secure both strands against your palm with your other fingers. Hold the slip knot in place with your right index finger. You can see why this is sometimes called the slingshot cast-on.

3

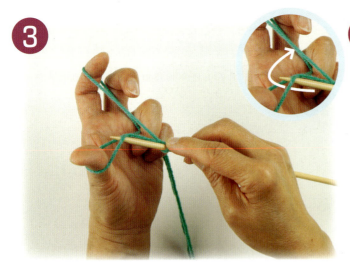

Insert the needle tip up through the loop on your left thumb from bottom to top, while continuing to hold the slip knot in place with your right index finger.

4

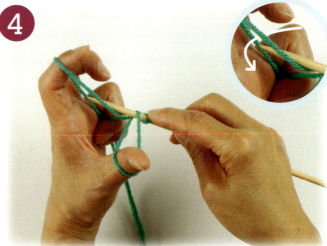

Rotate the needle tip clockwise, going over the top of the first strand on your index finger. Insert needle tip down into the index finger loop from top to bottom.

5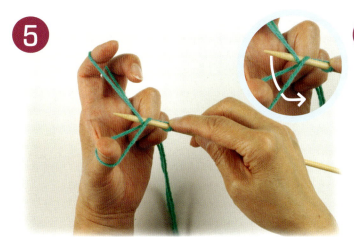

Rotate the needle tip counterclockwise, pulling the yarn from the index finger loop back through the thumb loop.

6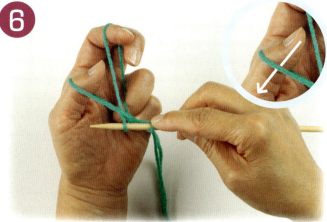

Drop your thumb out of the thumb loop. This will form a very loose loop.

7

Tighten the new loop on the needle by pulling the yarn tail and working yarn with your left thumb and index finger, forming a new cast-on stitch.

8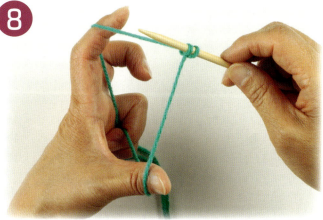

There are 2 loops on your needle (slip knot + cast-on stitch just made = 2 cast-on stitches). Repeat steps 2–7 for each additional cast-on stitch until reaching the required number of cast-on stitches.

Tip: Unlike with the knitted cast-on method, which uses two needles and adds cast-on stitches to the left-hand needle, the long-tail method uses only one needle held in the right hand. That means you'll need to switch the "full" needle with cast-on stitches to your left hand and hold an "empty" needle in your right hand when starting the next row.

Cable Cast-On

The cable cast-on is very similar to the knitted cast-on. The difference between the methods occurs after the first stitch is made. Like the knitted cast-on, the cable cast-on is especially good when you need a firm edge. Don't pull the stitches too tight or you will have a hard time getting the needle back into those cast-on stitches for the next row.

1

Start with a slip knot on the left needle. The empty needle and working yarn (the yarn coming from the ball) are on the right.

2

Insert the right needle through the stitch (the slip knot) on the left needle. The needles should form an X, with the right needle under the left needle. Hold the yarn tail out of the way against the needle with your left hand. Working yarn is on the right.

3

Wrap the working yarn around the right needle tip from back to front and bottom to top, ending between the needles.

4

With the right needle, draw that working yarn back through the slip knot, creating a new loop on the right needle. The left needle is now under the right needle. Insert the left needle tip into the new loop on the right needle, transferring the loop to the left needle.

Tip: To prevent the cast-on edge from becoming too tight, insert the right needle from front to back between the 2 stitches on the left needle before tightening yarn. Gently pull the working yarn to tighten the stitch.

5

There are 2 loops on your left needle (slip knot + cast-on stitch just made = 2 cast-on stitches).

6

Insert the right needle into the space between the 2 stitches on the left needle. The needles should form an X, with the right needle under the left needle.

7

Wrap the working yarn around the right needle as you did in step 3.

8

With the right needle, draw that working yarn back through the space to create a new loop on the right needle.

9

Insert the left needle tip into the new loop on the right needle, transferring the loop to the left needle. Repeat steps 6–9 until reaching the required number of cast-on stitches.

Tip: After using the cable or knitted cast-on method, you don't need to switch the needle to your left hand. The "full" needle with the cast-on row is already in your left hand and the "empty" or working needle is already in your right hand.

Backward Loop Cast-On

The backward loop cast-on (sometimes called the simple cast-on) is probably easiest to learn, but doesn't have a neat edge. This method is best when only working a few cast-on stitches. As it grows longer, it becomes less manageable.

1

Start with a slip knot on the right needle, holding the yarn tail out of the way against the needle. Wrap the working yarn behind your left index finger and around your left thumb, securing the yarn strand in your palm.

2

Insert the needle tip under and up through the yarn looped around your thumb and index finger.

3

Lift the needle up as you gently remove your left thumb and index finger. Pull the working yarn to tighten the new stitch on the needle.

4

There are 2 loops on the needle (slip knot + cast-on stitch just made = 2 cast-on stitches). Repeat steps 1–3 for each additional cast-on stitch until reaching the required number of cast-on stitches.

Tip: For methods that use one needle in your right hand like the backward loop cast-on, you'll switch the "full" needle with cast-on stitches to your left hand and hold an "empty" needle in your right hand before starting the next row.

How to Hold the Yarn

Knitting is enjoyed all over the world, but not everyone likes to knit in the same style. There is no right or wrong style of knitting. The two predominant knitting styles are English (sometimes called "throwing") and Continental (sometimes called "picking"). Both styles of knitting create the same end product; the only difference is which hand holds the working yarn (the yarn coming from the ball). English knitters hold the working yarn in the right hand, while Continental knitters hold the yarn in the left hand. This book presents the English method and is intended for right-handed knitters.

English

1

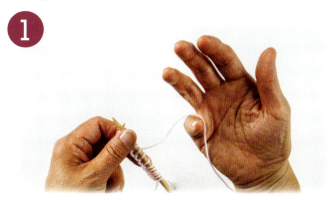

With your right palm facing up, weave the working yarn between your pinky and ring fingers. Wrap the yarn clockwise around your pinky.

2

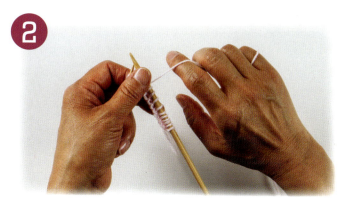

Turn your hand so your palm faces down. Bring the yarn under your ring and middle fingers. Then wrap the yarn over and around your index finger.

Continental

1

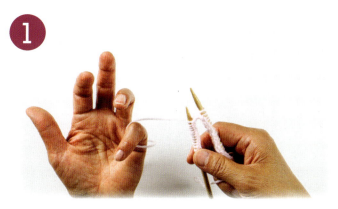

With your left palm facing up, weave the working yarn between your pinky and ring fingers. Wrap the yarn clockwise around your pinky.

2

Turn your hand so your palm faces down. Bring the yarn under your ring and middle fingers. Then wrap the yarn over and around your index finger.

How to Hold the Needles

There are also different ways to hold the knitting needles. Some knitters prefer to hold the needles over the top, while others hold the needles like pencils. Experiment until you find what works best for you.

Knit (k)

The knit stitch is the most common and versatile stitch. It's smooth on one side and bumpy on the other. The smooth side of knit stitch is generally used as the right side of the work—the side that faces out. The working yarn is always held behind the needle when making knit stitches.

Hold the needle with the cast-on stitches in your left hand. The working yarn is already attached to the stitch closest to the left needle tip. Hold the working yarn behind the empty needle in your right hand.

With working yarn behind, insert the right needle from front to back through the first cast-on stitch on the left needle (closest to the tip). The needles should form an X, with the right needle under the left needle.

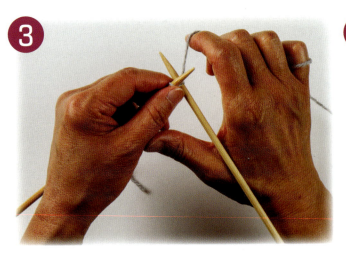

With your right hand, bring the working yarn from behind the needles toward the tip of the right needle. Next you will wrap the working yarn around the right needle.

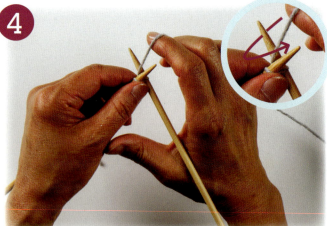

Wrap the working yarn clockwise around the right needle from back to front and bottom to top, ending between the needles.

5

With the right needle, draw that yarn back through the cast-on stitch on the left needle to form a new loop on the right needle.

6

slip st off left needle tip

Slip the cast-on stitch off the tip of the left needle.

7

You have completed 1 knit stitch. Unlike the knitted cast-on, the new knit stitches accumulate on the right (or working) needle.

8

Repeat steps 2–7 until all cast-on stitches have been knit from the left needle and are on the right needle. (This image shows the step before for the final cast-on stitch is slipped off the left needle.)

9

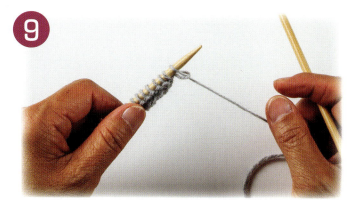

To start the next row, turn your work so the opposite side faces up. Switch the "full" needle with stitches to your left hand and the "empty" needle to your right hand. The working yarn is attached to the stitch closest to the tip, and held behind the empty right needle. Repeat the steps across the row, working into each of the stitches of the previous row rather than into the cast-on stitches.

> Tip: Before beginning each new row, make sure the working yarn is coming out of the bottom bump of the stitch closest to the left needle tip.

Purl (p)

The purl stitch is the reverse of the knit stitch. The working yarn is always held in front of your work when making purl stitches. As you work this stitch, the bumpy side faces you and the side behind the needle is now the smooth side.

Hold the needle with the cast-on stitches in your left hand. The working yarn is already attached to the stitch closest to the left needle tip. Hold the working yarn and the empty needle in your right hand. The working yarn should be in front, on top of the empty needle.

With the working yarn in front, insert the right needle through the front loop of the first stitch on the left needle (closest to the tip). The needles should form an X, with the right needle in front and the left needle behind.

With your right hand, bring the working yarn between the needles and toward the tip of the right needle. Next you will wrap the working yarn around the right needle (as directed in the inset).

Wrap the working yarn counterclockwise around the right needle, ending in front. Be careful not to wrap the yarn around the left needle.

5

Draw the right needle and the working yarn backward and away from you through the stitch on the left needle, forming a new loop on the right needle.

6

slip old st off left needle tip

Slip the old stitch off the tip of the left needle.

7

You have completed 1 purl stitch.

8

Repeat steps 2–7 until all cast-on stitches have been purled from the left needle and are on the right needle.

9

To start the next row, turn your work so the opposite side faces up. Switch the "full" needle with stitches to your left hand and the "empty" needle to your right hand. The working yarn is attached to the stitch closest to the left needle tip.

10

With working yarn held in front, repeat the steps across the row, working into each of the stitches of the previous row rather than into the cast-on stitches.

Garter Stitch

Knitting or purling every row in flat, back-and-forth knitting creates garter stitch. Garter stitch is a great stitch pattern for new knitters because it uses only one simple stitch. Garter stitch looks the same on both sides and is characterized by garter ridges. Because garter stitch lies flat and doesn't curl at the edges, it's often used at the beginning and end of rows to create a flat piece.

At the end of each row of garter stitch (or any other stitch), the right needle will be "full" and the left needle will be "empty."

Before starting the new row, turn your work so the opposite side faces up. Hold the "full" needle in your left hand and the "empty" needle in your right hand. Working yarn is held behind because we are knitting every row.

How to Make Garter Stitch:

Cast on the required number of stitches using your preferred method.

Row 1: Knit (or purl) in each stitch.

Repeat row 1 until reaching desired size.

> Tip: If you knit in the round, either with circular or double-pointed needles, knitting or purling each round will create stockinette stitch instead of garter stitch.

Stockinette Stitch (St st)

Alternating rows of knit and purl in flat, back-and-forth knitting makes stockinette stitch, in which the knit side is the right side (outward-facing) and the purl side is the wrong side (inward-facing). The bumpy, purl side of stockinette stitch is called reverse stockinette stitch, which uses the purl side as the right side and the knit side as the wrong side. Stockinette stitch is the most commonly used stitch pattern. Simply knit one row, purl the next, and repeat. Stockinette stitch tends to curl at the edges when not stabilized with other, non-curling stitch patterns, such as garter stitch. Because of that, border stitch patterns are usually added to the lower and upper edges, and side edges are sewn into the seam.

The smooth, knit side of stockinette stitch (St st)

The bumpy, purl side

When you start a knit row, make sure the working yarn is in back, behind the right needle.

When you start a purl row, make sure the working yarn is in front, on top of the right needle.

How to Make Stockinette Stitch:

Cast on the required number of stitches using your preferred method.

Row 1: Knit in each stitch.

Row 2: Purl in each stitch.

Repeat rows 1 and 2, alternating knit and purl, until reaching desired size.

Tip: There are several other stitch patterns included in this book. See page 38 for more stitch patterns.

21

Bind Off (BO)

Binding off (also called casting off) finishes the last row so the needles can be removed without your stitches unraveling. "Bind off in pattern" means work the last row of stitches as instructed, and bind off as you work. If a pattern doesn't say how to bind off, assume you should bind off knitwise (kwise) from the right side. Some patterns will instruct you to bind off purlwise (pwise), either because the right side of your work is the purl side or because the pattern calls for you to bind off on the wrong side.

Bind Off Knitwise

Begin with the right side (knit side) of your work facing up on the left needle.

Knit 2 stitches. There are 2 stitches on the right needle.

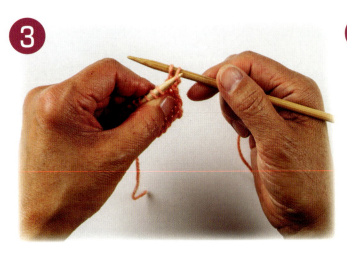

Insert the left needle tip from left to right into the front loop of the first stitch made on the right needle (the one farther from the right needle tip).

Use the left needle to lift this stitch over the second stitch made and drop it off the right needle tip.

5

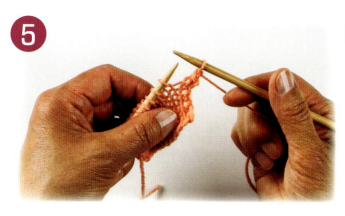

One stitch is bound off; one stitch remains on the right needle.

6

Knit the next stitch. There are 2 stitches on the right needle. Repeat from step 3 until you have bound off all stitches from the left needle and 1 stitch remains on the right needle. Then follow the fasten off instructions.

Bind Off Purlwise

1

Begin with the purl side of work facing up on the left needle.

2

Purl 2 stitches. There are 2 stitches on the right needle.

3

Insert the left needle from left to right into the back loop of the first stitch made on the right needle (the one farther from the right needle tip). Lift this stitch over the second stitch and drop it off the right needle tip.

Tip: Many new knitters tend to bind off too tightly. The bound-off edge should be as elastic as the rest of the knitting. If necessary, use a larger needle size to work the stitches in your bind-off row.

4

One stitch is bound off; one stitch remains on the right needle.

5

Purl the next stitch. There are 2 stitches on the right needle. Repeat from step 3 until you have bound off all stitches from the left needle and 1 stitch remains on the right needle. Then follow the fasten off instructions.

Fasten Off

After binding off, fasten off to secure the knitting.

1

Remove the right needle so the loop remains open.

2

Trim the working yarn, leaving a yarn tail a few inches long.

3

Pull the yarn tail from back to front through the loop until it fits snugly against the knitting.

Join New Yarn

When you near the end of a ball of yarn, try to change to the new yarn at the row edge. This will prevent the stitches in the middle of your work from becoming uneven, and it will make weaving in the yarn tails much easier because you can hide them in the seams. However, you won't have a row edge when knitting in the round. Just follow the instructions for joining new yarn in the middle of a row.

At the Beginning of a Row

1

Insert the right needle into the first stitch on the left needle (as if to knit in our example). Make a slip knot with the new yarn and place it on the tip of the right needle.

2

Draw through a loop using the new yarn rather than the old working yarn.

3

Continue stitching with the new yarn as usual. Make sure you're using the working yarn and not the tail of the new yarn.

> Tip: The first loop made with the new yarn will be very loose. Don't worry about that now. You can pull the yarn tail to tighten later.

In the Middle of a Row

To join new yarn in the middle of a row or anywhere in a continuous round, insert the right needle into the next stitch on the left needle. Make a slip knot with the new yarn and place it on the tip of the right needle. Draw through a loop using the new yarn rather than the old working yarn. Continue stitching with the new yarn as usual.

Changing Colors

When changing colors somewhere other than the end of a row, drop the old color on the wrong side, pick up the new color from underneath the old, and continue knitting with the new color. This prevents a hole from appearing between colors.

Weave in the Tail

Carefully weaving in the yarn tails makes your knitting look neat and keeps it from pulling loose and unraveling over time. Yarn tails can be woven into the cast-on edge, the bound-off edge, or the side (selvedge) edge for knitted items like scarves or blankets. For knitted garments, weave the yarn tails invisibly into the body of your work. Always weave in the yarn tails on the wrong side (the inward-facing or back side) of the knitting so it won't show on the right side (the outward-facing or front side). Cut the excess yarn close to your knitted piece when done weaving in the tails, being careful not to cut the actual knitting.

Along the Side (Selvedge) Edge

With the wrong side facing you, thread the yarn tail into the large eye of a tapestry needle.

Insert the needle from front to back through the first loop along the side (selvedge) edge, close to where you ended knitting, and draw yarn through. Insert the needle from back to front through the next loop and draw yarn through.

Continue weaving the needle through the loops along the side edge. Pull the yarn tail gently to tighten, and cut it close to your work when you're done weaving in the tail.

Tip: Weaving in the tail along the cast-on or bound-off edge works the same way as along the side (selvedge) edge. The only difference is where you're weaving in the tail.

Diagonally in the Body of the Work

Thread the yarn tail into a tapestry needle. Working on the wrong side, weave the needle diagonally through the bumps or loops of stitches, working one loop at a time.

Continue weaving the needle diagonally through the back or bottom loops to hide the yarn. Gently pull the yarn to tighten.

After you've done one part of the diagonal line, turn the knitting. This image shows the first diagonal already done and the knitting already turned.

Weave the needle through the bumps or loops of stitches in the opposite diagonal for a couple inches. Cut the yarn tail close to your work when done.

Tip: Make sure you're weaving in the tail on the wrong (or back) side. The garter stitch piece in our example looks the same on both sides, so it doesn't have an obvious right side and wrong side. Check the right side periodically while weaving in the tail to ensure no puckering occurs on the front.

Slip a Stitch

Slipping a stitch simply means moving the stitch from the left needle to the right needle without knitting or purling. This can be done as if to knit or as if to purl (knitwise or purlwise), and with the working yarn in back or in front (wyib or wyif). Pattern instructions usually indicate whether to slip the stitch purlwise or knitwise, and where the working yarn should be held.

Slip a Stitch as if to Purl/Slip 1 Purlwise (sl1p)

"Slip a stitch as if to purl" and "slip 1 purlwise" mean the same thing. It's more common to slip a stitch purlwise than knitwise. In fact, when a pattern instructs you to "slip 1" (abbreviated "sl1"), it's a safe bet it actually means to slip 1 purlwise (or sl1p). Insert your right needle into the next stitch as if you are going to purl it. Then transfer the stitch from the left needle to the right needle in its original, untwisted position. This means that the front loop of the stitch remains in front before and after it is slipped.

Slip a Stitch as if to Purl With Yarn in Front

slipped stitch
remains untwisted

With working yarn in front, insert the right needle tip into the next stitch on the left needle as if to purl (purlwise).

Slide the stitch off the left needle and onto the right needle. The slipped stitch remains untwisted.

Slip a Stitch as if to Purl With Yarn in Back

1. Bring the working yarn between the needles from the front to the back so that it's behind the right needle as shown on left. Ordinarily working yarn would be in front before a purl.

2. With working yarn in back, insert the right needle tip into the next stitch on the left needle as if to purl (purlwise).

3. Slide the stitch off the left needle and onto the right needle. The slipped stitch remains untwisted.

Slip a Stitch as if to Knit/Slip 1 Knitwise (sl1k)

Slipping a stitch as if to knit and slipping 1 knitwise (or sl1k) describe the same thing. You'll insert your right needle into the next stitch on the left needle as if you are going to knit it. Then slide the stitch from the left needle to the right needle. Notice that slipping a stitch knitwise results in the slipped stitch being transferred in a twisted position. The back loop of the stitch becomes the front loop, and the front loop becomes the back loop. Some stitch patterns require this.

With working yarn in back, insert the right needle tip into the next stitch on the left needle as if to knit (knitwise).

Slide the stitch off the left needle and onto the right needle.

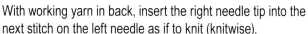

slipped stitch is twisted

The slipped stitch was twisted in the process, so the back is now the front and vice versa.

Where to Hold the Yarn

Patterns usually specify the location of the working yarn when slipping a stitch—either with yarn in back (wyib) or with yarn in front (wyif). Ordinarily you don't want the working yarn strand or float from the slipped stitch to show on the right side of your work. Therefore, the working yarn is typically in back when slipping a stitch on a right-side (RS) row. Conversely, the working yarn is typically in front when slipping a stitch on a wrong-side (WS) row. However, some stitch patterns reverse the normal process, so always follow the instructions carefully.

A rule of thumb: Always slip as if to purl (with yarn in front) unless the pattern instructions specify otherwise. An exception to this rule is that you'll always slip as if to knit when the stitch is part of a decrease method. A stitch that's part of a decrease is transferred to the right needle as if to knit, in the twisted position, because it will later become untwisted when the decrease is complete.

Increases (inc)

To increase, work multiple stitches into the same stitch. Increases shape your knitting and create lace patterns. There are many ways to make an increase; we've listed a few standard methods. Many patterns specify which type of increase to use; others do not. It's important to learn how each increase affects the appearance of your work. Practice all increasing techniques on a swatch before trying them on a project.

Knit Front and Back (kfb) Increase

Also known as the bar increase, the knit front and back increase is achieved by knitting into the same stitch twice—once in the front loop and a second time in the back loop. The knit front and back increase (abbreviated kfb, kf&b, or k1fb) is one of the easiest to make. It's also one of the most visible in stockinette stitch: It leaves a little bump that looks like a purl. Use it decoratively or when the purl bump is part of a stitch pattern.

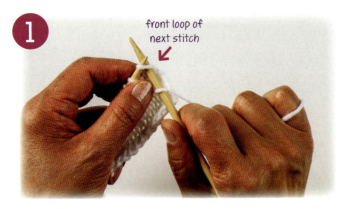

front loop of next stitch

With working yarn in back, insert the right needle into the front loop (the loop closer to you, on the front side) of the next stitch on the left needle as you would normally to knit.

don't remove · **1 knit made**

Wrap the yarn around the right needle and pull through a loop to make a knit stitch as usual, but don't remove the old stitch from the left needle. You will work into the back loop (the loop farther from you) of this same stitch next.

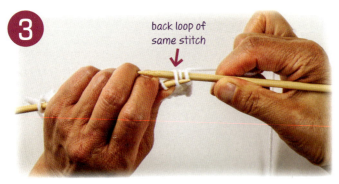

back loop of same stitch

Insert the right needle from right to left into the back loop (on back side) of the same stitch just worked as shown. Wrap the yarn around the right needle and pull through a loop to make another knit stitch in the back loop.

completed kfb

Slip the old stitch off the left needle. You have now completed a knit front and back increase, knitting into the same stitch twice (in the front and back loop), thus creating 2 knit stitches in place of 1.

Tip: Avoid making increases and decreases in the edge stitches, because they make it more difficult to make a smooth seam when finishing. Make increases or decreases at least 1 stitch in from the edge.

Purl Front and Back (pfb) Increase

The purl front and back increase (abbreviated pfb, pf&b, or p1fb) is accomplished by purling into the same stitch twice—once in the front loop and a second time in the back loop. It is the purl equivalent of the knit front and back increase, but a little less intuitive. This increase is most often used on the wrong (or purl) side but can be used on the right (or knit) side as well.

With the working yarn in front, insert the right needle into the front loop (the loop closer to you, in front) of the next stitch on the left needle as you would normally to purl.

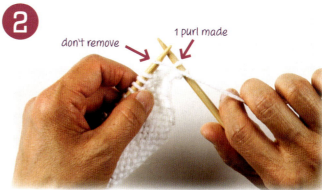

Wrap the yarn around the right needle and pull through a loop to make a purl stitch as usual, but don't remove the old stitch from the left needle. You'll work into the back loop of this same stitch in the next step. Keeping yarn in front, bring the right needle behind the left needle as shown.

Insert the right needle from left to right and back to front into the back loop (the loop farther from you, on the back side) of the same stitch just worked. Wrap the yarn around the right needle and pull through a loop to make another purl stitch in the back loop as shown.

Slip the old stitch off the left needle. You have completed a purl front and back increase, purling into the same stitch twice (in the front and back loop), thus creating 2 purl stitches in place of 1.

Tip: If you don't move to the back loop on the second purl of the pfb increase, you'll end up with a hole in your knitting that looks like a yarn over increase.

Make 1 (M1) Increases

These increases are made by working into the horizontal bar (or strand) between stitches on the right and left needles. One method creates a left-leaning increase, meaning that the front strand of the increase slants to the left. The other method leans to the right. These are called paired increases. Make 1 increases can be created with knit or purl stitches, although knit stitches are more common.

Make 1 Right-Leaning (M1R) Increase

Work to the position for the M1R increase. You'll work the knit stitch into the horizontal bar between the stitches on the needles. Next you will insert the left needle under the bar from back to front.

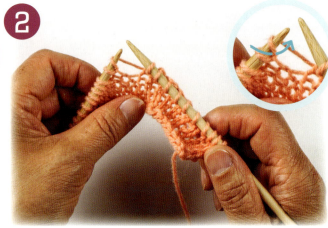

Insert the left needle from back to front under the horizontal bar, thus lifting it onto the left needle. This creates a short diagonal strand on the front of the left needle and a long horizontal strand behind. Next you will insert the right needle tip from left to right into the front strand on the left needle tip.

Insert the right needle from left to right through the strand on the front of the left needle, twisting to prevent a hole. Wrap yarn around the right needle and complete the knit stitch.

slip off left needle tip to complete

Slip the strand off the left needle. You will have 1 new stitch (an increase) on the right needle. The front strand leans toward the right.

Make 1 Left-Leaning (M1L) Increase

Work to the position for the M1L increase. Insert the left needle from front to back under the horizontal bar between stitches on the needles, thus lifting it onto the left needle. This creates a long diagonal strand on the front of the left needle and a short horizontal strand behind.

Insert the right needle from right to left through the strand on back of the left needle as shown, twisting to prevent a hole. Wrap yarn around the right needle and complete a knit stitch. Slip the strand off the left needle. You will have 1 new stitch (an increase) on the right needle. The front strand leans left.

Yarn Over (yo) Increase

The yarn over increase is quick and easy to make. In fact, many new knitters make yarn overs by accident. The yarn over increase leaves a visible hole in your work and is the basis for most lace patterns. To complete a yarn over increase, simply bring the working yarn to the opposite side of your work as it had been on (from back to front or from front to back). This creates an extra loop of yarn when you complete the next stitch. Our example shows a yarn over increase in stockinette stitch on a knit row.

Work to the position for the yo increase. Bring the working yarn between the needles to the front.

With yarn in front, knit in the next stitch.

Knit the next stitch. Notice that the yarn over increase has made an extra loop above the hole on the right needle that will be worked as a stitch on the next row.

On the next row, work into the extra yarn over loops as you would any other stitch.

Decreases (dec)

Decrease by working 2 stitches together at the same time. Use decreases for shaping necklines, making lace patterns, and more. Some decreases have a definite slant either left or right; pattern instructions may specify which type to use. Left- and right-slant decreases are called paired decreases. Avoid making decreases in the edge stitches.

Knit 2 Together (k2tog) Decrease

The knit 2 together decrease leans to the right on the knit side.

insert into next 2 stitches

Work to the position for the k2tog decrease, starting at least 1 stitch in from the edge. Next you will insert the right needle into the next 2 stitches on the left needle.

With working yarn in back, insert the right needle knitwise (as if to knit) into the next 2 stitches on the left needle. The needles should form an X, with the right needle under the left needle.

slip these 2 stitches off left needle

Knit these 2 stitches together at the same time as if they were 1 stitch: Wrap yarn around right needle as when knitting, draw yarn through both stitches to form a new loop on the right needle as shown, then slip the stitches off the left needle.

completed k2tog

You have completed a k2tog decrease. There is now 1 stitch on the right needle in the place of 2 stitches.

Purl 2 Together (p2tog) Decrease

As the name suggests, this decrease is the purl-side counterpart of the knit 2 together. The purl 2 together leans to the right when viewed from the knit side.

1

insert into next 2 stitches

Work to the position for the p2tog decrease. Next you will insert the right needle into the next 2 stitches on the left needle.

2

With working yarn in front, insert the right needle purlwise (as if to purl) into the next 2 stitches on the left needle. The needles should form an X, with the right needle on top and the left needle behind.

3

slip these 2 stitches off left needle

Purl the 2 stitches together at the same time as if they were 1 stitch: Wrap yarn around right needle as when purling, draw yarn through both stitches to form a new loop on the right needle as shown, then slip the stitches off the left needle.

4

completed p2tog

You have completed a p2tog decrease. There is now 1 stitch in the place of 2 stitches.

Slip Slip Knit (ssk) Decrease

The slip slip knit method is a 1-stitch decrease that leans to the left and is usually paired with knit 2 together on knit rows. This decrease is similar to k2tog except that ssk is worked through the back loops of 2 stitches at a time.

1

Work to the position for the ssk decrease. You will slip the next 2 stitches from the left needle onto the right needle.

2

first stitch slipped onto right needle

Slip 2 stitches knitwise (as if to knit), one at a time, from the left needle onto the right needle.

3

You now have 2 slipped stitches on the right needle. Next you will insert the left needle into the front loops of both slipped stitches.

4

Insert the left needle tip from left to right into the front loops of the 2 slipped stitches on the right needle.

5

completed ssk

Wrap the yarn around the right needle and with yarn in back, knit these 2 stitches at the same time through the back loops as if they were 1 stitch. You have completed a ssk decrease.

Slip Slip Purl (ssp) Decrease

The slip slip purl method is a 1-stitch decrease made on purl (wrong-side) rows. When viewed from the right side, it leans to the left and matches the slip slip knit, which is made on knit (right-side) rows. The slip slip purl is usually paired with purl 2 together on wrong-side rows.

1 Work to the position for the ssp decrease. The working yarn is in front because you're purling. You will slip the next 2 stitches from the left needle onto the right needle.

2 Slip 2 stitches knitwise (as if to knit), one at a time, from the left needle onto the right needle. The base of both stitches will be twisted at this point.

3 Once both stitches have been slipped onto the right needle, you will slip both stitches back to the left needle in their twisted position.

slip back to left needle

4 Bring the right needle behind the slipped stitches and insert right needle tip through back loops of both stitches from left to right, entering the second stitch first and then the first stitch.

5 Wrap the yarn around the right needle and with yarn in front, purl these 2 stitches together through the back loops at the same time as if they were 1 stitch.

6 You have completed a ssp decrease.

completed ssp

Seed Stitch

Seed stitch is a texture stitch pattern that alternates between knit and purl stitches within the same row. Whenever you're alternating between knit and purl, remember to bring the working yarn between the needles to the back before knit stitches and between the needles to the front before purl stitches. Both sides of seed stitch look the same.

To make this seed stitch pattern, cast on any odd number of stitches using your preferred method.

Row 1:

With the working yarn in back, insert the right needle knitwise into the first stitch on the left needle as shown and complete 1 knit stitch.

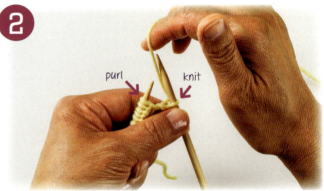

Bring the working yarn between the needles to the front as shown, on top of the right needle. Insert the right needle purlwise into the next stitch and purl 1.

Bring the working yarn between the needles to the back, behind the right needle as shown. Insert the right needle knitwise into the next stitch and knit 1.

Bring the working yarn between the needles to the front, on top of the right needle as shown. Insert the right needle purlwise into the next stitch and purl 1.

5

At the end of this and all subsequent rows, turn your work so that the opposite side faces up, the full needle with stitches is in your left hand, and the empty needle is in your right hand.

Continue repeating knit 1, purl 1 across the row, ending with a knit stitch.

Row 2:

1

purl

With the working yarn in front, insert the right needle purlwise into the first stitch on the left needle and complete 1 purl stitch.

2

Bring the working yarn in back, insert the right needle knitwise into the next stitch as shown, and knit 1. Continue repeating purl 1, knit 1 across the row, ending with a purl stitch.

At the end of this and all subsequent rows, turn your work so the opposite side faces up, the full needle is in your left hand, and the empty needle is in your right hand.

Repeat rows 1 and 2 to continue the pattern. Bind off in pattern.

Tip: In seed stitch, always do the opposite of what the next stitch on the left needle looks like. When you see the "V" of a knit stitch, purl. When you see the bump of a purl stitch, knit.

Tip: If the last row started and ended with knit stitches, the next row will start and end with purl stitches. If the last row started and ended with purl stitches, the next row will start and end with knit stitches.

Single Rib

Ribbing is an elastic pattern often found at the cuffs and hems of garments. The stitches in ribbing line up in vertical columns, with knit stitches directly above knit stitches and purl stitches directly above purl stitches. The single rib is made by alternating 1 knit stitch with 1 purl stitch. As with seed stitch, remember to bring the working yarn between the needles to the back for knit stitches and to the front for purl stitches. If you finish a row and discover extra stitches, or find a hole in the ribbing several rows later, it may be because you knit with yarn in front or purled with yarn in back.

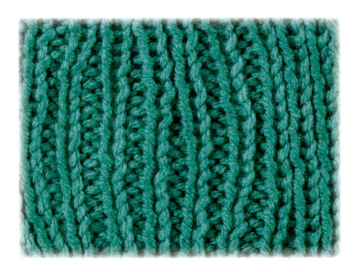

To make this single rib pattern, cast on any odd number of stitches.

Row 1:

With the working yarn in back, behind the needle, insert the right needle knitwise into the first stitch on the left needle as shown and complete 1 knit stitch.

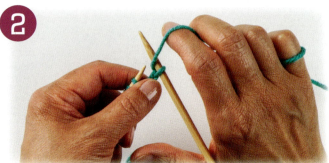

Bring the working yarn between the needles to the front, on top of the right needle as shown. Insert the right needle purlwise into the next stitch and purl 1.

Bring the working yarn between the needles to the back, behind the right needle as shown. Insert the right needle knitwise into the next stitch and knit 1.

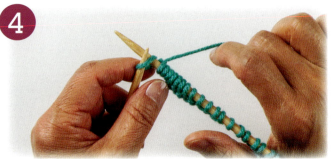

Continue repeating knit 1, purl 1 to the end of the row, ending with a knit stitch.

At the end of this and all subsequent rows, turn your work so that the opposite side faces up, the full needle is in your left hand, and the empty needle is in your right hand.

Row 2:

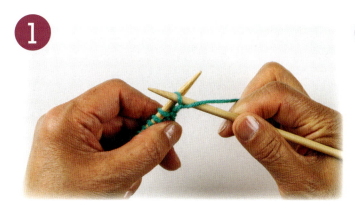

1 With the working yarn in front, on top of the right needle, insert the right needle purlwise into the first stitch as shown and purl 1.

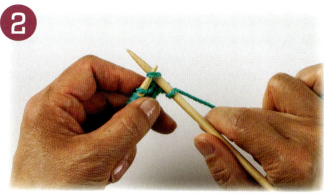

2 Bring the working yarn between the needles to the back, behind the right needle. Insert the right needle knitwise into the next stitch as shown and knit 1.

3 Continue repeating purl 1, knit 1 to the end of the row, ending with a purl stitch.

At the end of this and all subsequent rows, turn your work so that the opposite side faces up, the full needle is in your left hand, and the empty needle is in your right hand.

Repeat rows 1 and 2 to continue the pattern. Bind off in pattern.

Tip: Ribbing is easy once you learn to recognize knit and purl stitches. Knit stitches look like a "V"; purl stitches look like a bump. Simply knit the knit stitches and purl the purl stitches.

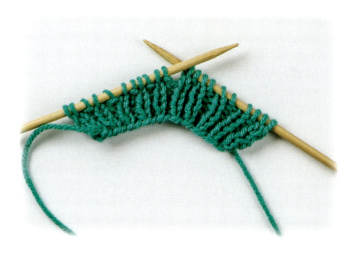

Double Rib

Double rib is more elastic than single rib. The double rib is made by alternating 2 knit stitches with 2 purl stitches. Knit 2 stitches, bring the working yarn between the needles to the front, purl 2 stitches, then bring the working yarn between the needles to the back before repeating.

To make this double rib pattern, cast on a multiple of 4 stitches.

Row 1:

1 With the working yarn in back, behind the needle, insert the right needle knitwise into the first stitch on the left needle as shown and complete 1 knit stitch. Complete another knit stitch for a total of 2.

2 After you knit 2, bring the working yarn between the needles to the front, on top of the right needle.

3 With the working yarn in front, insert the right needle purlwise into the next stitch, and purl 1. Complete another purl stitch for a total of 2.

4 Bring the working yarn between the needles to the back as shown, then knit 2. Bring the working yarn between the needles to the front, then purl 2. Continue repeating knit 2, purl 2 to the end of the row, ending with 2 purl stitches.

At the end of this and all subsequent rows, turn your work so that the opposite side faces up, the full needle is in your left hand, and the empty needle is in your right hand.

Row 2:

1

With the working yarn in back, knit the first 2 stitches.

2

After you knit 2, bring the working yarn between the needles to the front, on top of the right needle as shown. With the working yarn in front, purl the next 2 stitches.

Continue repeating knit 2, purl 2 to the end of the row, ending with 2 purl stitches. At the end of this and all subsequent rows, turn your work so the opposite side faces up, the full needle is in your left hand, and the empty needle is in your right hand.

Repeat row 1 to continue the pattern. Bind off in pattern.

> Tip: As you complete more rows, your knit and purl stitches will become easier to recognize. Knit the knits (the V-shapes) and purl the purls (the bumps).

Simple Cable

Make cables by working stitches out of order. Slip a set of stitches temporarily onto a cable needle (cn), and hold at the front or back as directed while you work another set of stitches. Then work the stitches on the cable needle. This moves the cable needle stitches left or right, creating a twisted effect.

To make this cable stitch pattern, cast on a multiple of 6 stitches (30 stitches in our example).

Row 1:

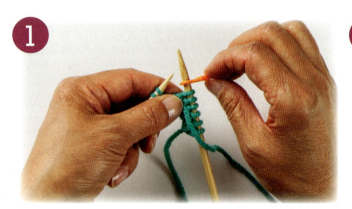

With working yarn in front, purl in the first 6 stitches. Place a stitch marker on the right needle tip as shown.

Bring the working yarn in back, and knit the next 6 stitches. Add another stitch marker on the right needle.

Bring the working yarn in front, and purl the next 6 stitches. Add another stitch marker.

Bring working yarn in back, then knit 6. Add another stitch marker as shown.

5

Bring the working yarn in front, then purl 6 to complete the row.

Tip: When switching between knit and purl stitches, remember to bring the working yarn to the front before purl stitches and to the back before knit stitches.

At the end of this and all subsequent rows, turn your work so that the opposite side faces up, the full needle is in your left hand, and the empty needle is in your right hand.

Row 2:

1

With working yarn in back, knit the first 6 stitches. When you reach the first stitch marker, slip the marker from the left needle onto the right needle as shown.

2

Bring the working yarn in front, then purl 6. Slip the marker onto the right needle. Repeat knit 6, purl 6 across the row, ending with knit 6.

At the end of this and all subsequent rows, turn your work so that the opposite side faces up, the full needle is in your left hand, and the empty needle is in your right hand.

Rows 3, 5: Repeat row 1: purl 6, knit 6, purl 6, knit 6, purl 6.

Rows 4, 6: Repeat row 2: knit 6, purl 6, knit 6, purl 6, knit 6.

Row 7 (cable row):

1

With working yarn in front, purl 6. Remove the next stitch marker from the left needle.

2

Bring out a cable needle. Make sure working yarn is in back, behind the needle.

3

slip onto cn

Slip the next stitch on the left needle onto a double-pointed cable needle (cn).

4

Repeat for the next 2 stitches so a total of 3 stitches are slipped onto the cable needle.

5

Push the 3 stitches into the curve of the cable needle.

6

With the cable needle in front and the working yarn in back, knit the next 3 stitches on the left needle before the next stitch marker.

7

Remove the next stitch marker once you reach it. Slip the 3 stitches on the cable needle back onto the left needle.

8

Release the cable needle completely. There should now be 9 stitches on the left needle before the next stitch marker.

9

purl next 6 stitches

Knit the next 3 stitches on the left needle (the same ones just slipped from the cable needle). By knitting the previous 6 stitches out of order, you create a twisted effect. Bring the working yarn between the needles to the front, then purl the next 6 stitches.

10

Remove the next stitch marker. With working yarn in back, slip the next 3 stitches from the left needle onto the curve of the cable needle. With cable needle in front and working yarn in back, knit the next 3 stitches.

11

Slip the 3 stitches from the cable needle back onto the left needle. Release the cable needle completely.

12

With working yarn in back, knit the next 3 stitches on the left needle (the same ones just slipped from the cable needle).

Rows 8, 10, 12: Repeat row 2: knit 6, purl 6, knit 6, purl 6, knit 6.

Rows 9, 11, 13: Repeat row 1: purl 6, knit 6, purl 6, knit 6, purl 6.

Row 14 (cable row): Repeat row 7.

Repeat rows 8–14 to continue the pattern. Bind off in pattern.

13

purl final 6 stitches

After you knit 6, bring the working yarn in front, then purl the final 6 stitches to complete the row.

Knit in the Round

Instead of working back and forth in rows to create a flat piece, work in rounds to create a continuous tube. Knit (or purl) in rounds to make hats, the body of seamless sweaters, leg warmers, and socks. To work in rounds, use either circular or double-pointed needles rather than straight (or single-point) needles.

With Circular Needles

Circular needles consist of two single-point needles connected by a cord. Circular needles come in various lengths (measured from tip to tip). Patterns will usually tell you the circular needle length to use.

Length	Common Uses
9" (23 cm)	Socks, mittens, cuffs
16" (40 cm)	Hats, small bags, sleeves
24" (60 cm)	Children's sweater bodies, tote bags
29" (74 cm)	Children's sweater bodies, small adults' sweater bodies
32" (80 cm)	Small adults' sweater bodies, small blankets
36" (91 cm)	Medium adults' sweater bodies, adults' shawls, medium blankets
40" (101 cm)	Medium and large adults' sweater bodies, large blankets

1

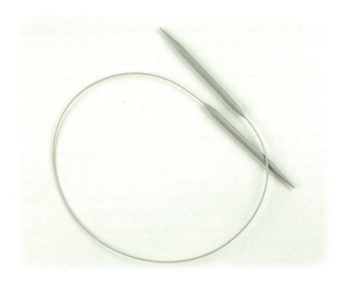

Cast on the required number of stitches the same way you would on straight needles. Make sure all the bumps of the cast-on stitches are facing the center of the circle and are not twisted.

2

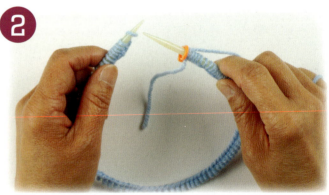

Hold the needle with the last cast-on stitch and working yarn in your right hand and the needle with the first cast-on stitch (slip knot) in your left hand. Add a circular stitch marker on the right needle tip to mark the beginning of the round.

3

Insert the right needle into the first stitch on the left needle as if to knit (knitwise) as shown. Complete the knit stitch as usual. You will have 1 completed knit stitch on the right needle after the stitch marker.

4

Continue making 1 knit stitch in each cast-on stitch, ensuring the visible cast-on edge stitches always face the center without twisting. The stitch marker will travel as you go.

5

Work around until you reach the stitch marker. At the end of round 1, slip the stitch marker from the left needle onto the right needle.

6

Work rounds 2 and on in the same way, or according to pattern instructions. Every time you reach the stitch marker, another round has been completed. Slip the stitch marker to the right needle tip and begin the next round.

> Tip: Work stockinette stitch and garter stitch in the round the opposite way you would in flat, back-and-forth knitting. For stockinette stitch in the round, work every round in knit stitch. For garter stitch in the round, alternate knit and purl rounds.

Knit Flat with Circular Needles

You can also use circular needles for flat, back-and-forth knitting. This is especially useful for large items like blankets and shawls with many stitches that won't fit on a straight needle. Cast on just as you would with straight needle(s). Think of the circular needle as two regular (straight) needles connected by a cord. At the end of each row, simply turn your work so that the opposite side faces up and continue stitching as you would with straight needles.

With Double-Pointed Needles (dpn)

Evenly distribute your cast-on stitches among 3 or 4 double-pointed needles (dpn). The needles either form a triangle (if you cast on 3 needles) or a square (if you cast on 4 needles). You'll need one additional needle with which to knit (so 4 or 5 needles total). Be sure the cast-on lies flat and smooth, and that no stitches are twisted. When moving from needle to needle, pull the working yarn tightly for the first stitch of each new needle to avoid gaps in your work.

1

Cast the same number of stitches onto each of 3 double-pointed needles (15 stitches on each needle in our example for a total of 45) using preferred method. We used the backward loop cast-on.

2

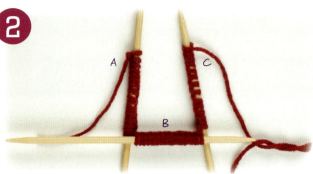

Lay the needles flat in a triangle shape that points up. The first stitch cast on (slip knot) should be on the top left (needle A). The last stitch cast on and working yarn should be on the top right (needle C). Make sure all cast-on edge stitches face the center of the triangle without twisting.

3

Take out a 4th double-pointed needle. This empty, free needle (D) will serve as the right-hand working needle initially. Insert needle D into the first cast-on stitch on needle A as if to knit.

4

Complete the knit stitch. New stitches will accumulate on the free, working needle (D). Place a stitch marker in the first stitch made on needle D. Stitch markers easily fall off the ends of dpn, so placing them in a stitch is more secure.

5

Continue making 1 knit stitch in each cast-on stitch on needle A. Once all stitches have been knitted from needle A onto needle D, A will become the new free needle.

6

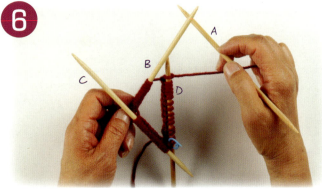

When needle A is empty, it becomes the new free needle. Hold the free needle (A) in your right hand and use it to knit the stitches on the next needle (B).

7

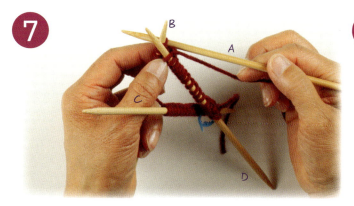

Insert the free needle (A) knitwise into the next stitch on the next needle (B) as shown and complete the knit stitch. Knit all stitches from needle B onto needle A. When needle B is empty, it becomes the new free needle and is used to knit the stitches on the next needle (C). Continue around until you reach the stitch marker.

8

To start a next round, insert the free needle knitwise (or as instructed) into the stitch with the marker. After completing the new stitch, move marker from old stitch to new stitch. Work rounds 2 and on the same way, or according to pattern instructions. Move stitch marker up after completing the first stitch of every new round.

Bind Off in the Round

Bind off in the round with circular or double-pointed needles. The process is the same as with straight needles in flat, back-and-forth knitting until the final step. Binding off is demonstrated below with double-pointed needles. Unlike knitting in the round with double-pointed needles where the free needle changes, you'll use the same free needle throughout the binding off process.

1

Using the free right-hand needle, knit the first 2 stitches on the left-hand needle. You have 2 knit stitches on the free needle as shown. Next you will insert the left-hand needle from left to right into the front loop of the first stitch you knit (farther from tip), then lift it over and off the free needle.

2

lift st over and off

When you have 2 stitches on the free needle, skip the 2nd stitch you knit (closer to tip) and insert the left needle from left to right into the front loop of the first stitch (farther from tip) on the free needle. Lift this stitch over the 2nd stitch and drop it off the free needle. One stitch is bound off; one stitch remains on the free needle. Knit the next stitch.

3

Repeat step 2 until 1 stitch remains on the left-hand needle. Follow step 2 instructions again, but stop after lifting first stitch over 2nd stitch (shown) and dropping it off free needle, when 1 stitch remains on the free needle.

4

knit next stitch

You have eliminated 1 needle; 2 needles remain in addition to the free needle. Knit the next stitch on the left. Repeat steps 2–3 across the left needle.

5

Continue this process until end of round when only the free needle remains. Notice the dip where the stitch marker is, between the bound-off stitches on the left and the right.

6

Remove the stitch marker. Insert the needle from front to back into the very first stitch made, which is lower.

7

Wrap the working yarn around the needle as shown, and draw that yarn through both the first stitch and the loop on the right needle.

8

One loop remains on the needle as shown. Remove the needle so the loop remains open. Trim working yarn, leaving a tail a few inches long. Pull yarn tail from back to front through the loop until it fits snugly.

Tip: To bind off in the round with a circular needle, follow the same process as with straight needles until you reach the marker and 1 stitch remains on the right needle, then follow steps 5–8 above.

Fix Mistakes

One thing to know about knitting mistakes is that we all make them. You'll inevitably twist, drop, or accidentally create extra stitches. Fortunately, knitting is easily corrected, and you'll learn from any missteps along the way. Once you learn to correct them, you'll be happily on your way again.

Fix a Twisted Stitch

It's important to recognize the correct orientation of a stitch. Knit and purl stitches form a loop or upside-down U on the needle. Imagine the stitch is a gymnast on a balance beam, looking off to the right: Her right leg is in front of the beam; her left leg is behind. Similarly, the right or leading leg of a stitch should be in front of the needle, while the left leg should be behind the needle. When a stitch is twisted, the right leg is behind and the left leg is in front.

twisted stitch

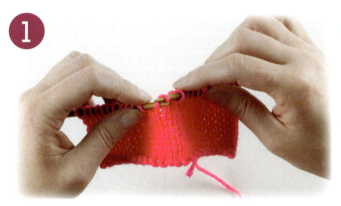

To fix a twisted stitch, insert the right needle into the twisted stitch from behind.

Slide the stitch loop off the left needle.

Place the stitch loop back onto the left needle with the correct orientation.

Fix Dropped Stitches

If your stitch count is less than it should be, it may be because a stitch has dropped from the needle. A crochet hook is the best tool to correct a dropped stitch. Before fixing a dropped stitch, count the horizontal strands between the two needles to determine how many rows the stitch has dropped. Each loose horizontal strand equals one row.

Fix a Dropped Knit Stitch

Fix a dropped knit stitch with the right (or knit) side facing you. Be sure the dropped stitch loop is in front and the loose horizontal strand(s) behind.

Insert the crochet hook from front to back into the dropped stitch loop and then under the very first horizontal strand closest to the dropped stitch. Catch that first horizontal strand with the hook.

Pull that horizontal strand through the dropped stitch loop. One dropped stitch has been picked up.

Repeat with each horizontal strand until the dropped stitch is back at the current row.

Place the stitch on the left needle untwisted, with the right leg of the stitch in front of the needle. Continue in pattern.

Fix a Dropped Purl Stitch

Fix a dropped purl stitch from the wrong (or purl) side. Be sure the dropped stitch loop is behind and the loose horizontal strand(s) in front. **To fix a dropped purl stitch:** Coming from behind your work, insert the crochet hook from back to front into the dropped stitch loop and then under the first horizontal strand closest to the dropped stitch. Catch that horizontal strand with the hook, and pull up through the dropped stitch loop. You have 1 loop on the crochet hook. Repeat with each horizontal strand until the dropped stitch is back at the current row. Place the stitch on the left needle in the correct, untwisted position. Continue in pattern.

Avoid Extra Stitches

An increasing stitch count is a common complaint of new knitters. This happens because of how the working yarn is handled when you finish the last stitch of a row, then turn your work to start the next row.

Incorrect: When turning your work to begin a new row, don't bring the working yarn over the top of the needle and pull it down on the back side. This moves the bump at the bottom of the stitch over the top of the needle, creating 2 loops instead of 1.

Correct: To avoid creating this extra loop, make sure the working yarn is exiting the bump at the bottom of the stitch underneath the needle before starting a new row. Make a habit of pulling the working yarn down and away from the needle at the end of every row.

Un-Knit

Un-knit (sometimes called tink, which is knit spelled backward) to take out a stitch or even multiple rows of stitches to correct a mistake. This process reverses what happened to stitches on the right needle.

1

To un-knit a stitch, insert the left needle from front to back through the center of the stitch in the row below the stitch on the right needle (the hole from which the loop on the right needle is exiting).

2

While keeping the left needle in the stitch below, remove the right needle from the stitch on the needle. The stitch loop that was closest to the right needle tip now hangs free.

Pull the working yarn gently out of the stitch. Repeat steps 1–3 as many times as necessary.

3

Tip: If you need to un-knit several rows, remove the needle completely from your work. Gently pull the working yarn to unravel your work row by row until reaching the point one row above the stitch(es) needing correction. Return the live stitches to the needle and un-knit stitch by stitch following steps 1–3.

Pick Up Stitches

Sometimes you'll need to "pick up stitches" to add a border or an extra section to a knitted piece that has already been finished. Pick up stitches using a knitting needle or crochet hook and new yarn. Work with the right side of the piece facing up, unless instructed otherwise.

Along a Bound-Off Edge

Make a slip knot with new yarn. With right side facing up, insert the right needle from front to back into the first stitch in the bound-off row (in the top right corner).

Place the slip knot on the tip of the needle and pull a loop up to the front. The slip knot will catch on the back.

Insert the needle from front to back into the next stitch to the left, going under both loops of the stitch along the edge.

Wrap the yarn around the needle on back, and pull another loop up to the front as shown.

Continue inserting the needle from front to back into the next stitch to the left, wrapping working yarn around the needle tip on back (shown), then pulling a loop up to the front. You'll add another loop to the needle each time you pick up a stitch.

Repeat for each stitch until the required number of stitches have been picked up and are on the needle (shown). Then turn your work so the wrong side faces up and continue pattern instructions.

Along a Side (Selvedge) Edge

1

Make a slip knot with new yarn. With right side facing up, insert the right needle from front to back into the first stitch of the first row along the side (or selvedge) edge.

2

Follow bound-off edge steps 2–6, working along the side edge and occasionally skipping a row to space the pickup stitches as necessary. After the required number of stitches have been picked up (shown), turn your work so the wrong side faces up and continue pattern instructions.

Tip: For a neater edge, use needles or a hook one or two sizes smaller than the working needle. After the pickup is finished, change to the needle size indicated in the instructions.

Tip: The steps are the same for picking up stitches along a cast-on, bound-off, or side (selvedge) edge; the only difference is where you're working. Typically, 1 stitch should be picked up for each stitch along a cast-on or bound-off edge. Because knit stitches are wider than they are tall, stitches should be picked up along the side edge at a ratio of about 3 stitches for every 4 rows or 5 stitches for every 7 rows.

Along a Curved Edge

Curved or sloping edges are usually a combination of horizontal, diagonal, and vertical edges. To pick up stitches along straight parts, use a circular needle and follow the same steps as with bound-off or side edges.

1

insert here

To pick up stitches along a diagonal edge formed by decreases, such as along a neckline, insert the needle into the stitch below and to the left of the edge stitch—not the hole between stitches.

2

After the required number of stitches have been picked up (shown), turn your work so that the wrong side faces up and continue pattern instructions.

Join with Seams

Block each piece before joining (or seaming) together. Blocking helps edges lie flat, makes joining easier, and forces your knitted project into the proper shape. **To block:** Mist knitted piece with spray water bottle until evenly saturated. Stretch damp item into desired shape on padded surface such as blocking board. Pin edges. Leave undisturbed until completely dry.

There are many joining/seaming techniques. Most patterns recommend a method; some do not. Make sure stitches in both pieces are correctly lined up before you start sewing seams. Thread a tapestry needle with matching yarn for seaming. (We used contrasting yarn in our examples for clarity.)

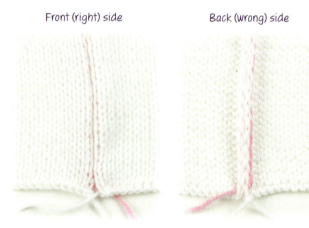

Front (right) side   Back (wrong) side

Backstitch

Backstitch is an easy way to make an extra strong, but bulky, seam. To join seams with backstitch, start by placing both pieces with right sides together and edge stitches lined up. Thread a tapestry needle with matching yarn.

1

Insert the threaded tapestry needle from front to back through the corner stitch of both pieces.

2

Draw the yarn through on the back, leaving a tail to weave in later.

3

Insert the needle from back to front through the next pair of stitches to the left. Draw the yarn through.

4

Insert the needle from front to back through the first pair of corner stitches again (the same place as in step 1) and draw the yarn through.

5

Skip the next pair of stitches to the left. Insert the needle from back to front through the next pair of stitches after the skipped stitches. Draw the yarn through.

6

Insert needle from front to back through the previous pair of stitches (the ones you skipped) and draw the yarn through.

7

Tip: When joining pieces with a backstitch or whipstitch seam, consider using safety pins or stitch markers to lock the beginning, middle, and ending stitches of both pieces together.

Repeat steps 5–6 across the seam. Weave in tails when done.

Whipstitch

To join with whipstitch, start by placing both pieces with right sides together and edge stitches lined up. Thread a tapestry needle with matching yarn. Use stitch markers to lock both pieces together at the beginning, middle, and end stitches.

Front (right) side   Back (wrong) side

Insert the threaded tapestry needle from front to back through the first pair of stitches on the right as shown. Draw the yarn through on the back, leaving a tail to weave in later.

Bring the tapestry needle over the top and insert from front to back through the next pair of stitches to the left.

Draw the yarn through on the back. Pull gently to tighten.

Repeat the process across the seam. Weave in tails when done.

Mattress Stitch

Mattress stitch (also called invisible stitch) creates seams that are flat and nearly invisible. Mattress stitch is great for sewing vertical seams in garments, including side and sleeve seams. To join with mattress stitch, place both pieces with right sides facing up and side edges lined up. Thread a tapestry needle with matching yarn.

Front (right) side   Back (wrong) side

1

Insert the threaded tapestry needle from back to front through the bottom corner stitch on the right-hand piece. Draw the yarn through, leaving a tail to weave in later. Insert the needle from back to front through the bottom corner stitch on the left-hand piece and draw through.

2

If you pull the knitted piece out to the side, you'll see a pair of little horizontal bars between the edge stitch and the 2nd stitch for each row. On the right-hand piece, insert the needle under the pair of bars above where last stitch was made on that side. Draw the yarn through.

3

Insert the tapestry needle under the corresponding pair of bars on the left-hand piece and draw the yarn through.

4

Continue working under the horizontal bars, alternating pieces, across the seam. Occasionally pull yarn to tighten. Weave in tails when done.

Tip: If the pieces you're seaming together are not exactly symmetrical, compensate by weaving the needle under 2 horizontal bars on the longer piece and 1 bar on the shorter piece.

I-Cord

Use an I-cord as a drawstring, strap, or tie. Make an I-cord with 2 double-pointed needles.

1

Cast 4 stitches onto a double-pointed needle using your preferred method, leaving a tail several inches long.

2

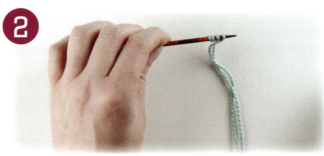

Rather than turning the full needle so that the opposite side faces up, to start a new row, slide the stitches from the left to the right end of the needle. The working yarn is now at the "wrong" end of the needle, on the left.

3

Insert the empty double-pointed needle in your right hand knitwise into the next stitch as shown. Pull the working yarn tightly behind the stitches from left to right, then over the top of the right needle tip, ending between the crossed needles. Complete the knit stitch. Knit the remaining 3 stitches.

4

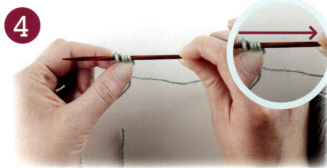

When you have knit all 4 stitches, start the next row. Rather than turning your work over, slide the stitches to the right end of the full needle. Hold the full needle in your left hand and the empty needle in your right hand. The working yarn should always be on the left side of the stitches on the full needle when starting a new row.

5

Repeat until the cord is the desired length. Unless instructed otherwise, bind off stitches and cut yarn, leaving a long tail with which to sew.

6

Finishing the I-cord: Thread the yarn tail through a tapestry needle. Draw the tail end through all the stitches on the needle twice, right to left. Drop all stitches from the needle and pull taut.

Gauge

Gauge refers to how many stitches (or rows) there are in a given area of knitting using a specific yarn and needle size. The pattern will state how many stitches and rows are needed to achieve the correct gauge. Remember, the needle size listed in the pattern is the size the designer used to obtain the listed gauge. Two knitters using the same materials may end up with different gauges.

Make Your Gauge Swatch

Using the main needle size and yarn recommended in the pattern, cast on about 6" of stitches. Work the main pattern until the swatch measures at least 4" in length. Bind off all stitches. Lay the swatch on a flat, hard surface.

Stitch gauge = 15 stitches to 4"

Measure Your Gauge Swatch

Using measuring tape or a ruler, measure and then count 4" of stitches horizontally across the swatch. Divide this number by 4 to get the number of stitches per inch. Repeat a few times in different areas to confirm the count. This is the stitch gauge.

To measure the row gauge, place the measuring tape or ruler lengthwise (vertically) on the swatch, and count the number of rows over 2" or 4" if the pattern is very large vertically. Divide the total by 2 (or 4, if using that measurement) to determine the number of rows per inch.

Row gauge = 22 rows to 4"

Adjust Your Gauge

Compare your gauge with the pattern gauge. If your gauge swatch has too many stitches or rows, try larger needles. If your swatch has too few stitches or rows, try smaller needles. Keep adjusting needle sizes until you obtain the correct gauge.

Tip: Knit stitches are wider than they are tall; however, in stitch patterns such as stockinette stitch, you'll normally have more rows per inch than stitches per inch.

Read a Knitting Pattern

Like most crafts, knitting has its own language. Knitting patterns use abbreviations, special terms, and punctuation. The language may seem strange at first, but you'll quickly master it. Instructions inside asterisks, brackets, or parentheses are usually repeated, so look for the directions that explain what to do.

Abbreviations

alt	alternate	**p2tog**	purl 2 stitches together; single decrease
approx	approximately	**prev**	previous
beg	begin/beginning	**pwise**	purlwise
bet	between	**rem**	remain/remaining
BO	bind off	**rep**	repeat(s)
CC	contrasting color	**rev St st**	reverse stockinette stitch
cm	centimeter(s)	**RH**	right hand
cn	cable needle(s)	**rnd**	round(s)
CO	cast on	**RS**	right side
cont	continue	**sl**	slip; slip 1 or more stitches from one needle to the other without working
dec	decrease; eliminate 1 or more stitches	**sl1k**	slip 1 knitwise
dpn	double-pointed needle(s)	**sl1p**	slip 1 purlwise
foll	follow	**sl st**	slip stitch
in. or "	inch(es)	**ssk**	slip slip knit: slip 2 stitches knitwise, knit these 2 stitches together through back loops; single left-leaning decrease
inc	increase; add 1 or more stitches	**ssp**	slip slip purl: slip 2 stitches knitwise, return these 2 stitches to left needle and purl them together through back loops; single left-leaning decrease
k	knit	**st(s)**	stitch(es)
kfb	knit front and back: knit 1 into front and back of a stitch; single knit increase	**St st**	stockinette stitch
k2tog	knit 2 stitches together; single right-leaning decrease	**tbl**	through back loop
kwise	knitwise	**tfl**	through front loop
LH	left hand	**tog**	together
lp	loop	**WS**	wrong side
M1 or M1K	make 1 stitch knitwise; single knit increase	**wyib**	with yarn in back
M1L	make 1 left; single left-leaning knit increase	**wyif**	with yarn in front
M1R	make 1 right; single right-leaning knit increase	**yd(s)**	yard(s)
MC	main color	**yo**	yarn over
oz	ounce(s)	*****	repeat instructions following the single asterisk as directed
p	purl	******	repeat instructions between asterisks as many times as directed or repeat at specified locations
pat or patt	pattern	**[ ]**	work instructions within brackets as many times as directed
pfb	purl front and back: purl 1 into front and back of a stitch; single purl increase	**( )**	work instructions within parentheses as many times as directed or work a group of stitches all in the same stitch or space